PANIC!

100 POEMS
TO SAVE YOUR LIFE

Don't Panic!

100 POEMS TO SAVE YOUR LIFE

Chosen by Fiona Waters

MACMILLAN CHILDREN'S BOOKS

For Deborah and Maureen with best love

First published 2003
by Macmillan Children's Books
a division of Macmillan Publishers Ltd
20 New Wharf Road, London N1 9RR
Basingstoke and Oxford
www.panmacmillan.com
Associated companies throughout the world

ISBN 0 330 41581 6

3 5 7 9 8 6 4 2

A CIP catalogue record for this book is available from the British Library.

Printed in China

Contents

Give Yourself a Hug

Give yourself a hug
when you feel unloved

Give yourself a hug
when people put on airs
to make you feel a bug

Give yourself a hug
when everyone seems to give you
a cold-shoulder shrug

Give yourself a hug—
a big big hug

And keep on singing,
'Only one in a million like me
Only one in a million-billion-thrillion-zillion
like me.'

Grace Nichols

Friendship

Friendship
Is precious
Keep it
Protect it
You will need it
Don't throw it away
Don't break it
Don't neglect it
Keep it
Somewhere
In your heart
If you want to
Somewhere in your thoughts
If you want to
But keep it
For, friendship

Has no borders
And its boundary
Is that of the world
It is the colour
Of the rainbow
And it has the beauty
Of a dream
Never listen
To those who say
It doesn't exist any more
It is here
It is yours
When you want it
All you have to do is:
Open
Your eyes

Veronique Tadjo

Don't Panic! 3

Friendship

If you're ever in a jam,
  Here I am.
If you're ever in a mess,
  S.O.S.
If you ever feel so happy you land in jail,
  I'm your bail.

It's friendship, friendship,
Just a perfect blendship.
When other friendships have been forgot,
Ours will still be hot.

If you're ever up a tree,
  Phone to me.
If you're ever down a well,
  Ring my bell.
If you ever lost your teeth and you're out to dine,
  Borrow mine.

Don't Panic!

It's friendship, friendship,
Just a perfect blendship.
When other friendships have been forgate,
Ours will still be great.

If they ever black your eyes,
  Put me wise.
If they ever cook your goose,
  Turn me loose.
If they ever put a bullet through your brain,
  I'll complain.

It's friendship, friendship,
Just a perfect blendship.
When other friendships have been forgit,
Ours will still be it.

Cole Porter

Don't Panic! 5

Friends Again

When snow melts to slush
And noise becomes hush,
When smile answers frown
And upside turns down,
When bitter tastes sweet
And both our ends meet
Then a flash in the pan
Will be what we began.

When each finds the other
And lose is discover,
When feeble feels strong
And short stretches to long,
When head rules the heart
And we make a fresh start,
Then if No or if Yes
Will be anyone's guess.

John Mole

Friends

I fear it's very wrong of me
And yet I must admit,
When someone offers friendship
I want the *whole* of it.
I don't want everybody else
To share my friends with me.
At least, I want *one* special one,
Who, indisputably,

Likes me much more than all the rest,
Who's always on my side,
Who never cares what others say,
Who lets me come and hide
Within his shadow, in his house –
It doesn't matter where –
Who lets me simply be myself,
Who's always, *always* there.

Elizabeth Jennings

I Know What I'm Missing

It's a birdcall from the treeline.
I hear it every day.
It's the loveliest of the songbirds
And I'm glad it comes this way
And I stop to listen
And forget what I've to do
And I know what I'm missing –
My friend
My friend.

It's a fluttering in the palm fronds
With a flash of black and gold.
It's the whistling of the oriole
And its beauty turns me cold
And I stop to listen
And forget what I've to do
And I know what I'm missing –
My friend
My friend.

Do you wonder if I'll remember?
Do you wonder where I'll be?
I'll be home again next winter
And I hope you'll write to me.
When the branches glisten
And the frost is on the avenue
I'll know what I'm missing –
My friend
My friend
I'm missing you.

James Fenton

A Little Health

A little health,
A little wealth,
A little house and freedom,
And at the end
A little friend
And little cause to need him.

Anonymous

From the diary of Francis Kilvert

Spell to Banish a Pimple

Get back pimple
get back to where you belong

Get back to never-never land
and I hope you stay there long

Get back pimple
get back to where you belong

How dare you take up residence
in the middle of my face

I never offered you a place
beside my dimple

Get back pimple
get back to where you belong

Get packing pimple
I banish you to outer space

If only life was that simple

John Agard

Why Won't She Listen?

My friend Mandy's fat but even
that's not her biggest problem
which is, she doesn't even care.

She's fat and plain from her
smooth round face with little
brown eyes to her podgy feet in
flat, battered shoes, size eights.

She won't put on make-up or spend
time on what she wears. I've never
even seen her glance into a mirror
checking on her hair. She won't diet
or come to Mum's gym with me to
work-out, do some re-structuring.
She is a *mess*. I tell her straight.

When I said I'd give her streaks
or do a perm she only grinned.
And said what she always says
that she's satisfied with being
the way she is. But she *can't* be!

I watch her when we're waiting for
the teacher in the morning. We all
stand round Mandy's chair to talk.
It's a shame! Poor Mandy, bulging
through the chair. She *should* care.

I do wish she'd listen, take my
advice. I really could help, offered
twice today but as usual didn't have
chance to say what I wanted to –
with people trying to get her to
agree to play chess, or talking
about soccer and other rubbish –
like a boring book they've all read.

If I go after school she's never
alone – she's a pretty good cook
has a darkroom at home. There's some
sort of camera club meets every month.
But I never go. They're all so boring!

Joan Poulson

Chocs

Into the half-pound box of Moonlight
my small hand crept.
There was an electrifying rustle.
There was a dark and glamorous scent.
Into my open, religious mouth
the first Marzipan Moment went.

Down in the crinkly second layer
five finger-piglets snuffled
among the Hazelnut Whirl,
the Caramel Swirl,
the Black Cherry and Almond Truffle.

Bliss.

I chomped, I gorged.
I stuffed my face,
till only the Coffee Cream
was left for the owner of the box –
tough luck, Anne Pope –
oh, and half an Orange Supreme.

Carol Ann Duffy

Against Dieting

Please, darling, no more diets.
I've heard the talk on why it's
good for one's esteem. I've watched you
jogging lanes and pounding treadmills.
I've even shed two kilos of my own.
But enough. What are love-handles
between friends? For a half a stone
it isn't worth the sweat.
I've had it up to here with crispbread.
I doubt the premise too.
Try to see it from my point of view.
I want not less but more of you.

Blake Morrison

The Pencil Test

To find out if you're firm and pert of breast
Or so the women's magazines all say
You really have to do 'the pencil test'
I'm told this is the only foolproof way.
You'd think, by looking, you could surely tell
And this old pencil lark seemed quite bizarre
But then one day I thought 'oh what the hell'
And recklessly removed my well-wired bra.
To my chagrin, the pencil stayed in place
Instead of dropping down on to the floor
I found this outcome somewhat hard to face;
I then tried with a felt pen to make sure.
I failed again and though I was displeased . . .
I found a handy place to keep HBs.

Judy Rose

Short Thought

I wish I had rings running through me like trees,
Then you'd know I wasn't lying about my age.

Elaine Cusack

The Mirror

Whenever I look in the mirror
I find that it's me who is there,
Wearing identical clothing
And staring straight into my stare.

I've tried creeping up without warning
And peeking from outside the frame.
But whatever I look like that day
Looks back – it's exactly the same.

I think, can I trick my reflection
And glimpse someone famous or rich?
A model or maybe a film star,
I really don't mind what or which.

Yet it's me who gets in the picture,
Always me in the glass gazing out;
Sleepy, untidy or grumpy.
But me. Absolutely. No doubt.

Steve Turner

Face in the Mirror

What am I? What am I? Tell me.
This pale dark rimmed face,
skin sallow, eyes underscored with purple bruises,
mouth too full, mouth too big
hair a black unruly ruff
I brush it slowly into a furry hood
holding the brush out after each stroke
to hear it retort wispily.
My eyes are darkly mournful,
an outside rim of black, then brown
around the black staring pupils.
My face is sick. I do not like it. It is not me.

Who am I? What am I? Tell me.
I have shed self after self
as a grasshopper swells
leaving dried brown leaves of bodies in the dust.
Inside each shield of self is the core,
alive, persistent, urged tropistically
toward light and warmth.
I lift myself like a blind worm
wondering which way next.

I have memorized many facts
but love none of them.
Forces stir in me.
I compress them until my brain boils.
I move uneasily in this thin awkward body
hitting against the back of my eyes
like moths against a lighted window.

Who am I? What am I? Tell me.

Marge Piercy

Mirror, Mirror

A young spring-tender girl
  combed her joyous hair
'You are very ugly,' said the mirror.
But,
    on her young lips hung
    a smile of dove-secret loveliness,
    for only that morning, had not
    the blind boy said,
    'You are beautiful'?

Spike Milligan

Brilliant Star

hand to its glass
a blind child questions
the windows blaze
      she listens
as the bushes dance
to the rhythm of a breeze
never to be life's prisoner,
nor ask who or why
her two dazzling blue eyes
celebrate every brilliant star

Robert 'Skip' Mills

Who Do You Think You Are?

Who do you think you are
and where do you think you came from?
From toenails to the hair of your head you are
      mixed of the earth, of the air,
Of compounds equal to the burning gold and
      amethyst lights of the Mountains of the Blood
      of Christ at Sante Fe.
Listen to the laboratory man tell you what you are
      made of, man, listen while he takes you apart.
Weighing 150 pounds you hold 3,500 cubic feet of
      gas – oxygen, hydrogen, nitrogen.
From the 22 pounds and 10 ounces of carbon in you
      is the filling for 9,000 lead pencils.
In your blood are 50 grains of iron and in the rest of
      your frame enough iron to make a spike that
      would hold your weight.

From your 50 ounces of phosphorus could be made
800,000 matches and elsewhere in your
physical premises are hidden 60 lumps of sugar,
20 teaspoons of salt, 38 quarts of water, two
ounces of lime, and scatterings of starch,
chloride of potash, magnesium, sulphur,
hydrochloric acid.
You are a walking drug store and also a cosmos and a
phantasmagoria treading a lonesome valley, one
of the people, one of the minions and
myrmidons who would like an answer to the
question, 'Who and what are you?'

Carl Sandburg

Don't Panic! 27

Depression

Came here
to write
a poem
on depression
but

got fed up
and left.

Steve Turner

Smile

Smile, go on, smile!
Anyone would think, to look at you,
that your cat was on the barbecue
or your best friend had died.
Go on, curve your mouth.
Take a look at that beggar,
or that one-legged bus conductor.
Where's *your* cross?
Smile, slap your thigh.
Hiccup, make a horse noise,
lollop through the house,
fizz up your coffee.
Take down your guitar
from its air-shelf and play
imaginary reggae
out through the open door.
And smile, remember, smile,
give those teeth some sun,
grin at everyone,
do it now, go on, SMILE!

Matthew Sweeney

New Leaf

Today is the first day of my new book.
I've written the date
and underlined it
in red felt-tip
with a ruler
I'm going to be different
with this book.

With this book
I'm going to be good.
With this book
I'm always going to do the date like that
dead neat
with a ruler
just like Christine Robinson.

With this book
I'll be as clever as Graham Holden,
get all my sums right, be as
neat as Mark Veitch;
I'll keep my pens and pencils
in a pencil case
and never have to borrow again.

With this book
I'm going to work hard,
not talk, be different –
with this book,
not yell out, mess about,
be silly –
with this book.

With this book
I'll be grown-up, sensible,
and everyone will want me;
I'll be picked out first
like Iain Cartwright:
no one will ever laugh at me again.
Everything will be
different

with this book . . .

Mick Gowar

Uniform

'You'll grow,' she said and that was that. No use
To argue and to sulk invited slaps.
The empty shoulders drooped, the sleeves hung
  loose –
No use – she nods and the assistant wraps.

New blazer, new school socks and all between
Designed for pea pod anonymity.
All underwear the regulation green;
Alike there's none to envy, none to pity.

At home she feasts on pins. She tacks and tucks
Takes in the generous seams and smiles at thrift.
I fidget as she fits. She tuts and clucks.
With each neat stitch she digs a deeper rift.

They'll mock me with her turnings and her hem
And laugh and know that I'm not one of them.

Jan Dean

Gillian Costigan

I wish I was Gillian Costigan,
with hair brushed sleek
and clothes that fit.
I wish I was Gillian Costigan
with money in my pocket every single week.

Her smile is wide,
her shoes have a shine,
she has friends to tea,
she laughs all the time.

I wish I was Gillian Costigan.
She has holidays in Greece,
her Dad loves her Mum,
she has nieces and nephews,
a Nan and a Gran,
her sarnies are thick
with hard cheese *and* ham.

I wish I was Gillian Costigan
with a slide in my hair,
a huge Mum to hug me,
a new top to wear.

Chrissie Gittins

Purple Shoes

Mum and me had a row yesterday,
a big, exploding
howdareyouspeaktomelikethatI'mofftostayatGran's
kind of row.

It was about shoes.
I'd seen a pair of purple ones at Carter's,
heels not too high, soft suede, silver buckles;
'No' she said
'Not suitable for school.
I can't afford to buy rubbish.'
That's when we had our row.

I went to bed longing for those shoes.
They made footsteps in my mind,
kicking up dance dust;
I wore them in my dreams across a shiny floor,
under flashing coloured lights.
It was ruining my life not to have them.

This morning they were mine.
Mum relented and gave me the money.
I walked out of the store wearing new purple
     shoes.
I kept seeing myself reflected in shop windows
with purple shoes on,
walking to the bus stop,
walking the whole length of our street
wearing purple shoes.

On Monday I shall go to school in purple shoes.
Mum will say no a thousand furious times
But I don't care.
I'm not going to give in.

Irene Rawnsley

Haircut

What I hate
about having a haircut
is being asked
how I want it
when I don't want it cut at all.

What I hate
about having a haircut
is being asked
questions with
the whole room listening to my answers.

What I hate
about having a haircut
is being asked
to look in
the mirror and say how I like it.

What I hate most
about having a haircut
is going to school
and everyone
telling me I've had my hair cut.

Michael Harrison

Visit to the Dentist

What a likkle cry baby!
Look how de bwoy a bawl,
One likkle injection him get,
Him no ha' no shame at all.

Ah bet him older than me, Mama,
But me wouldn' cry so loud,
In fac' me wouldn' cry at all
Especially eena crowd.

An look how people a look pon him,
Me shame fe him yuh see,
Me couldn' show me face again
If that likkle bwoy was me.

Eh eh, but look noh, Mama,
One other one a cry,
An the girl who a come out now
Water full up her yeye.

But feba something really wrong
Else them wouldn' frighten so
Mama, guess what happen,
Me toothache gone, yuh know.

The nurse a call we, Mama,
But a couldn' fe we time a'ready?
'Pickney before big people'
Mek the likkle girl go before me.

She go a'ready? A me one lef?
Nurse, tell the dentist noh fe bother,
Me toothache gone fe good now
Unless him want fe see me mother?

Mama, yuh wouldn' force me
An know how me fraid o'needle too,
No badda carry me een there,
Waia! Smaddy come help me, do!

Waia! Murder! Help! Police!
No mek him touch me, oh!
Me heart not too good, Doctor,
Me will dead from fright yuh know.

Don't Panic! 41

Wait, Mama, yuh hear that?
Him cyan do nutten when me gum swell soh,
So me mus tek some aspirin tonight
An come back come see him tomorrow.

This dentist is a nice man,
Him smile so sweet an warm,
What mek them pickney cry-cry soh?
Him wouldn' do them any harm.

Watch that one there still a bawl,
The pickney noh have no shame,
Me woulda never mek so much noise
(Me glad me get 'way today all the same).

Valerie Bloom

Driven to Distraction

I picked up a bus in the High Street
then put it down on the park,
I drove my Mum to Distraction –
that's the next town from Dunkirk.

I stood, like a lemon, in a downpour
and someone gave me a squeeze,
I gave the cold shoulder to Matthew,
in minutes it started to freeze.

I got into hot water for fibbing,
the water didn't tell me a thing,
I threw bread at a tree for a lark
but instead it decided to sing.

I turned up my nose at the dinner,
it stayed like that for a week,
I tried not to be a wet blanket,
but my shoelaces started to leak.

Chrissie Gittins

Sound Count Down

turn of a tap
clicking cap

pulled plug
clinked mug

slowing trickle
final gurgle

squirt of spray
towel put away

cupboard door squeak
basket creak

something picked off the floor
opening door—

can it be
the bathroom's free?

Robert Hull

My Room

It's only a room.
But it's my room.
My space, my base,
my place in the world.

Brown bears stare
from a ledge up above.
I don't play with them now
but can't give them the shove.
They're stuffed
too full of love.

On the floor:
a pair and a half
of socks,
a bundle of keys
without locks,
a pair of goggles
in a box.

My life story
is neatly filed, piled,
pinned and hung:
passport photos,
posters, paperbacks,
pop stars, playing cards,
programmes and
pieces of paper.

It's only a room.
But it's my room.
Somewhere to go,
somewhere to sleep,
somewhere to be sent,
somewhere to hide,
somewhere to cry,
somewhere to dress,
somewhere to think.
Somewhere to be.

Steve Turner

Blowin' in the Wind

How many roads must a man walk down
Before you call him a man?
Yes, 'n' how many seas must a white dove sail
Before she sleeps in the sand?
Yes, 'n' how many times must the cannon balls fly
Before they're forever banned?
The answer, my friend, is blowin' in the wind,
The answer is blowin' in the wind.

How many times must a man look up
Before he can see the sky?
Yes, 'n' how many ears must one man have
Before he can hear people cry?
Yes, 'n' how many deaths will it take till he
        knows
That too many people have died?
The answer, my friend, is blowin' in the wind,
The answer is blowin' in the wind.

Don't Panic! 47

How many years can a mountain exist
Before it's washed to the sea?
Yes, 'n' how many years can some people exist
Before they're allowed to be free?
Yes, 'n' how many times can a man turn his
    head,
Pretending he just doesn't see?
The answer, my friend, is blowin' in the wind,
The answer is blowin' in the wind.

Bob Dylan

The Void

Look into my face
And take a pace
Into a wilderness
Of driftwood, dunes and sand.
A no man's land.

Step inside my head,
Inspect the empty bed,
The room swept bare,
No clue. No mess.
No forwarding address.

Tune into my mind,
Rewind
The silent spools and brush
The bat-winged echoes from your hair.
I am not there.

Sue Cowling

Passage

Your history is a trap door
that you must struggle through
blinking from the darkness
into a shower of light.

Imtiaz Dharker

Walls

With no consideration, no pity, no shame,
they've built walls around me, thick and high.
And now I sit here feeling hopeless.
I can't think of anything else: this fate gnaws my
      mind –
because I had so much to do outside.
When they were building the walls, how could I
      not have noticed!
But I never heard the builders, not a sound.
Imperceptibly they've closed me off from the
      outside world

C. P. Cavafy

I cannot

I envy you.
At any moment
you can leave me.

But I cannot
leave myself.

Anna Swir

That's Life –
Or It Ought To Be

I am the sort of person who dogs bite
Of whom their owners say
'But she never bites *anyone*'.

And you, the other half I'd like to be
You come along as the bus draws up
And jump straight on.

I get to the town just as the cafes are closing.
You keep both gloves, together, in a drawer,
Or if you drop one, it's there when you go back.

Together we are called 'day', 'life' or 'it'
But life's hard on me when we are separate.

Jenny Joseph

Don't Panic! 53

Ring Home

She's come so far, what can she say?
She's punched her last coin in.
There's a pinball flicker
of connections, then the ansafone:

her mother, the voice
of her whole life so far
sounding cramped in that little
black box, speaking slow

as a hostage in the judder
of a ransom video. *Please
leave your name and your number.
Speak after the tone.*

She can't find the words to explain
to a ghost in a machine
a hundred miles away
in the hall in the house that was home.

Philip Gross

Going Too Far

Cuddling the new telephone directory
After I found your name in it
Was going too far.

It's a safe bet you're not hugging a phone book,
Wherever you are.

Wendy Cope

Love Between Two Cultures

Between two cultures you find
a love that is different,
Between two cultures you find peace and
friendship,
and when you fall in love
it doesn't matter of what blood, just the blood
that is in your heart.

Juan C. Medina Arias

Daily – Old Tale

If one's heart is broken twenty times a day,
What easier thing to fling the bits away,
But still one gathers fragments, and looks for
     wire,
Or patches it up like some old bicycle tyre.

Bicycle tyres fare hardly on roads, but the heart
Has a longer time than rubber, they sheath a cart
With iron; so lumbering and slow my mind must
     be made –
To bother the heart and to teach things and learn
     it its trade.

Ivor Gurney

Easy

He swaggers downstairs and stops
To see who might be looking, hesitates
And joins a group who loll against the wall;
Drags attention from a fag burn in the carpet
By dramatic adjusting of his shirt,
Then squats. 'Got a fag?' he asks,
Grinning deliberately, willing them
One of them, to ask: 'Where is she then?'
Only a slight exhalation indicates relief at being
    asked.
Slowly he draws a breath,
Like the drumroll preceding the high wire act
And rolls his eyes.
'Upstairs y'know, Sortin' herself out.'
And he smiles a lazy smile
And hooks his thumbs in belt loops,
Stage whispers, 'First time y'know: hers, not
    mine of course.'

And his audience lean back appreciatively.
'Where's that fag then? Gotta light?' Deep drag
      now.
'Well, yeah, bit of a slag, but a goer. Oh yeah! A
      real goer.'
They are reeled in, staring and envious
'Did you really?'
'Oh yeah, too right' . . .

While upstairs,
Mascara tears
Rain black
Into the basin.

Andrew Fusek Peters and Polly Peters

Oh, When I Was in Love

Oh, when I was in love with you,
  Then I was clean and brave,
And miles around the wonder grew
  How well did I behave.

And now the fancy passes by,
  And nothing will remain,
And miles around they'll say that I
  Am quite myself again.

A. E. Housman

Valentine

Not a red rose or a satin heart.

I give you an onion.
It is a moon wrapped in brown paper.
It promises light
like the careful undressing of love.

Here.
It will blind you with tears
like a lover.
It will make your reflection
a wobbling photo of grief.

I am trying to be truthful.

Not a cute card or a kissogram.

I give you an onion.
Its fierce kiss will stay on your lips,
possessive and faithful
as we are,
for as long as we are.

Take it.
Its platinum loops shrink to a wedding-ring,
if you like.

Lethal.
Its scent will cling to your fingers,
cling to your knife.

Carol Ann Duffy

DiVorce

I did not promise
to stay with you till death us do part, or
anything like that,
so part I must, and quickly. There are things
I cannot suffer
any longer: Mother, you have never, ever, said
a kind word
or a thank you for all the tedious chores I have done;
Father, your breath
smells like a camel's and gives me the hump;
all you ever say is:
'Are you off in the cream puff, Lady Muck?'
In this day and age?
I would be better off in an orphanage.

I want a divorce.
There are parents in the world whose faces turn
up to the light
who speak in the soft murmurs of rivers
and never shout.
There are parents who stroke their children's cheeks
in the dead of night
and sing in the colourful voices of rainbows,
red to blue.
These parents are not you. I never chose you.
You are rough and wild,
I don't want to be your child. All you do is shout
and that's not right.
I will file for divorce in the morning at first
        light.

Jackie Kay

Camera

freezing my smile
for half a second
I look
toward your camera
that can't photograph my heart.

Tawara Machi

Spared

*'That Love is all there is,
Is all we know of Love . . .' – Emily
Dickinson*

It wasn't you, it wasn't me,
Up there, two thousand feet above
The New York street. We're safe, and free,
A little while, to live and love,

Imagining what might have been –
The phone-call from the blazing tower,
A last farewell on the machine,
While someone sleeps another hour,

Or worse, perhaps, to say goodbye
And listen to each other's pain,
Send helpless love across the sky,
Knowing we'll never meet again,

Or jump together, hand in hand,
To certain death. Spared all of this
For now, how well I understand
That love is all, is all there is.

Wendy Cope

What Is That Word?

What is that word again?
It seems to have slipped my memory.
No one seems to remember it anymore
It's the opposite of war.
But I know that word well,
Guns, bombs and blood everywhere,
Yes, I know that word.
But what about the other word?
I even seem to remember it at night,
Flashes of green, black and red.
But what is that other word?
No one seems to know.

Meagan McManus

Latch Key

My best friend Danny comes to dinner with a
        key
round his neck, tied on with a piece of string.
At night when no one's home he lets himself in,
even though he is only seven, only seven.
My mum says he's too young and it's a shame.
He watches TV alone and eats crisps left for
        him.
And Mrs Robinson—the old woman next door—
listens out for him. Though my mum says,
she is hard of hearing. What does that mean?

Danny's mummy is always rushing off
        somewhere,
all dressed up to the nines and sometimes,
when the taxi comes she throws a kiss
like a piece of bread to a duck; it drops on our
        street
with a sigh. Then Danny scoops up his kiss
and comes into our house holding on to it.
Can Danny have a bath with me? I plead,
and my mum sighs yes, she supposes so,
because he is only seven, only seven.

Jackie Kay

Colour Blind

If you can see the sepia in the sun
Shades of grey in fading streets
The radiating bloodshot in a child's eye
The dark stains in her linen sheets
If you can see oil separate on water
The turquoise of leaves on trees
The reddened flush of your lover's cheeks
The violet peace of calmed sea

If you can see the bluest eye
The purple of petals of the rose
The blue anger, the venom, of the volcano
The creeping orange of the lava flow
If you can see the red dust of the famished road
The white air tight strike of Nike's sign
If you can see the skin tone of a Lucien Freud
The colours of his frozen subject in mime

If you can see the white mist of the oasis
The red, white and blue you defended
If you can see it all through the blackest pupil
The colours stretching, the rainbow suspended
If you can see the breached blue of the evening
And the caramel curls in the swirl of your tea
Why is it you say you are colour blind
When you see me

Lemn Sissay

Equal Opportunity

in early canada
when railways were highways

each stop brought new opportunities

there was a rule

     the chinese could only ride
     the last two cars
     of the trains

that is

until a train derailed
killing all those
in front

(the chinese erected an altar and thanked buddha)

a new rule was made

the chinese must ride
the front two cars
of the trains

that is

      until another accident
      claimed everyone
      in the back

(the chinese erected an altar and thanked buddha)

after much debate
common sense prevailed

the chinese are now allowed
to sit anywhere
on any train

Jim Wong-Chu

Survivor

Everyday
I think about dying.
About disease, starvation,
violence, terrorism, war,
the end of the world.

It helps
keep my mind off things.

Roger McGough

Cornered

They chased me to the corner of the playground,
Where the air is colder
Because spiteful gusts of wind rush at the
        chain-link fence,
And dust blows in your face, rubs like
        sandpaper.

One tear escaped – then all was lost.
In for the kill, their teeth flashed through parted
        lips,
Their eyes narrowed in contempt.
I stared at the tarmac, cornered.

Rhymed insults sang a sneering song around my
        head
And 'Baby! Baby! Baby!' boxed my ears
Until I was on the ground
My fingers spread over my face like prison bars.

Coral Rumble

Curse All Bullies

For bullies who hurt
with words that sting,
make them afraid
of harmless things.

May slugs keep them from their sleep,
May flies make their flesh creep;
May shadows give them a fearful shock,
May nits make their knees knock;
May starlings stand their hair on end,
May dragonflies drive them round the bend . . .

May butterflies betray them,
May damselflies dismay them.

May Sunday make them sad,
May Monday drive them mad;
May Tuesday give them a terrible time,
May Wednesday make them whine;
May Thursday give them tears,
May Friday give them fears;
May Saturday cause them pain,
Looking forward to Sunday again.

May frogs give them a fright,
May toads turn their hair white;
May chickens give them a chill,
May warts destroy their will;
May scabs make them scared,
May ducks make them despair;
May worms make them worry,
May hamsters make them hurry.

May snails subdue them,
May bugs bugaboo them.

For bullies who hurt
with words that sting,
make them afraid
of harmless things.

Mike Jubb

Overheard Conversation on the Way to School

He's been picking on me for ages now and
I've been taking it. Well, I'm not taking
it any more, so there.

The thing is I've had to have a talk to myself.
Ask myself why this guy can try and make fun
of me and my country

and I just let him. Interesting question.
Well, not any more. He's had it with me.
Next time, I'm ready

watch me soar high above him, my big
angry wings flapping *do you think it's funny
do you think you're better?*

Up there in the air he will get smaller
and smaller until he is the size of a pigeon
dropping, a smudge, a blot

on the playground. I'm not hanging around,
hands on my ears, eyes close to tears, any
longer. Come on. Try me.

Jackie Kay

Touchy

'WHO D'YOU THINK YOU'RE STARING AT?'
The bomber-jacket

on a short fuse
scans the disco crush

The can in his grip
makes a hush

as it crumples. Everybody
finds a different way

to look anywhere else,
not to lock on his eyes.

'WHO D'YOU THINK YOU'RE STARING AT?'
He really needs to know.

Any moment he'll be rattling
someone like a street-collector's tin

with only coppers in it. Then
he'll nut him, drop him limp

at our feet and stare round
at a loss for an answer.

Philip Gross

Bruises Heal

Names, cold shoulders,
Silence in the canteen;
Her words are scalpels,
Cutting self esteem.

'Stuck up little cow!
Thinks she's really it!'
Laughter slices, she prescribes
A sharp, unfunny wit.

Ridiculed for standing out,
My marks are much too high
And so she drip-feeds saline hate,
Injecting with a lie.

She's bright, she'll find
The weakest spot to pierce and prod and poke.
She uses stealth, and poisoned words
And wears them like a cloak.

It seems I am her favourite game
And I'm the one who loses,
If she'd done this with her fists,
At least there would be bruises.

Andrew Fusek Peters and Polly Peters

When you are called names, remember

If bullies mock and reject you
Repeat after the poet, please:
A cat's a wonderful creature
That does not converse with its fleas.

Brian Patten

Team Spirit

Oh no, not him, sir. He's no good.
I didn't ask to join their team.
I try, but I run out of steam
And let them down again. Dead wood.

The joys of sporting brotherhood
Are not for me. I spoil their scheme.
Oh no, not him sir. He's no good.
I didn't ask to join their team.

How many afternoons I've stood
And heard the P.E. master scream
What's up, lad! Are you in a dream?

I wish I was. I wish I could.
But this is real and I'm no good
And Hell is being in a team.

Wendy Cope

Bringing Up a Single Parent

It's tough bringing up a single parent.
They get really annoyed when they can't stay
    out late,
or when you complain about them acting soppy
over some nerdy new friend,
(even though you are doing it for their own
    good).
It's exhausting sometimes, the way you have to
    please them,
and do things you absolutely hate while
    pretending
it's exactly what you want.
Yep. Bringing up a single parent
is a real chore.
You don't get extra pocket money for them,
or special grants,
and you have to get up in the morning
and allow them to take you to school
so they can boast to their friends
about how clever you are.
And what's worse,

you have to allow them to fret over you,
otherwise they get terribly worried.
And if you are out doing something interesting
        after school
you have to keep popping home all the time
to check they're not getting up to any mischief
with a new friend, or smoking, or drinking too
        much.
You have to try and give single parents
that extra bit of attention.
But once you've got them trained,
with a bit of patience and fortitude
they're relatively easy to look after
Still, it can be tough
bringing up a single parent.

Brian Patten

Get Your Things Together, Hayley

Mum said the dreaded words this morning,
'Get your things together, Hayley,
We're moving.'

I've at last made a friend, and Mrs Gray
Has just stopped calling me
The New Girl.

Why do we have to go now
When I'm just beginning
To belong?

It's OK for my sister,
She's good with people.
They like her.

But I can't face the thought
Of starting all over again,
In the wrong uniform,

Knowing the wrong things,
In a class full of strangers
Who've palled up already

And don't need me.
Mum says, 'It's character-forming, Hayley.'
I say it's terribly lonely.

Frances Nagle

Monotony

One monotonous day follows another
identically monotonous. The same things
will happen to us again and again,
the same moments come and go.

A month passes by, brings another month.
Easy to guess what lies ahead:
all of yesterday's boredom.
And tomorrow ends up no longer like tomorrow.

C. P. Cavafy

playground haiku

Everyone says our
playground is overcrowded
but I feel lonely

Helen Dunmore

Crab-apples

My mother picked crab-apples
off the Glasgow apple trees
and pounded them with chillies
to change
her homesickness
into green chutney.

Imtiaz Dharker

Balloonland

In Balloonland
everyone
is given a balloon
the day they are born.

Freshly blown-up
and with the knot tightly done,
a big balloon
is put into their hand.

A few words are spoken
by way of ceremony:
'This is your balloon,
the balloon of your destiny!
You are its guardian.
Do you understand?'

And it's no use arguing.
Red, blue or green,
yellow, purple or orange,
that's their balloon
and no one else's.
They are the owner.

So as time goes on
they watch their balloon
with increasing anxiety.
Can it be shrinking?
Is it less shiny?
What's that hissing sound?
Did they do something wrong?

Futile questions!
Some balloons
pop the day they are given,
others last aeons
just getting more wizened.
If you're looking for a reason,
goes one of the Balloonland's
wisest sayings
then apply your own pin.

Christopher Reid

Broken Moon

for Emma

Twelve, small as six,
Strength, movement, hearing,
all given in half measure,
my daughter,
child of genetic carelessness,
walks uphill, always.

I watch her morning face;
precocious patience as she hooks each sock,
creeps it up her foot,
aims her jersey like a quoit.
My fingers twitch;
her private frown deters.

Her jokes can sting:
'My life is like dressed crab
– lot of effort, rather little meat.'
Yet she delights in seedlings taking root,
finding a fossil,
a surprise dessert.

Chopin will not yield to her stiff touch;
I hear her cursing.
She paces Bach exactly,
firm rounding of perfect cadences.
Somewhere inside
she is dancing a courante.

In dreams she skims the sand,
curls toes into the ooze of pools,
leaps on to stanchions.
Awake, her cousins take her hands;
they lean into the waves,
stick-child between curved sturdiness.

She turns away from stares,
laughs at the boy who asks
if she will find a midget husband.
Ten years ago, cradling her,
I showed her the slice of silver in the sky.
'Moon broken,' she said.

Carol Satyamurti

a quiet daughter

they found me in the corner
way at the back
of my mother's wardrobe

at first they thought i was a button
broken loose from a frayed thread
or a mothball, happy in the dark

then, as i grew, they thought i was
a shoe without a partner, but
they were busy folk – it was easier
to poke me back beside the fallen
jumpers and the missing socks

as for me, i was quite content
tucked up in the folds of mother's frocks

from time to time she'd drag me out
wear me, dangled prettily
on the end of her arm –
the ultimate accessory
a quiet daughter

Magi Gibson

Poem For My Sister

My little sister likes to try my shoes,
to strut in them,
admire her spindle-thin twelve-year-old legs
in this season's styles.
She says they fit her perfectly,
but wobbles
on their high heels, they're
hard to balance.

I like to watch my little sister
playing hopscotch, admire the neat hops-and-
    skips of her,
their quick peck,
never-missing their mark, not
over-stepping the line.
She is competent at peever.

I try to warn my little sister
about unsuitable shoes,
point out my own distorted feet, the callouses,
odd patches of hard skin.
I should not like to see her
in my shoes.
I wish she would stay
sure footed,
    sensibly shod.

Liz Lochhead

Climbing the World

Heading home, the faces
of the passengers opposite
are reflected dark blue
in the late night train windows.

I doze, my daughter yawns.

The head of the sleeping man
next to me lolls about like a puppet's.
His paperback slips from his lap
and falls onto the orange peel
he discarded before falling asleep.

He wakes in time to get off at Sevenoaks.

I pick up the book, brush the peel off the jacket.
It's *The Diary of a Young Girl: Anne Frank,*
the '97 Penguin edition, due back
at Paddington Library by 13 Dec.
I start reading the foreword

. . . Anne Frank kept a diary . . .

Her father, Otto Frank, edited her diaries
after she was dead.
I see him crying at the typewriter.

My daughter is 27.
We have great times together.
She is my friend and I love her.
Even in a train's harsh light she is very
       beautiful.
She is climbing the world.

Anne and Otto Frank
have taught me how to tell you this.

I shall now return the sleeping man's
book to Paddington Library.

John Rice

Don't Panic!

Father's Hands

Father's hands
large like frying pans
broad as shovel blades
strong as weathered spades.

Father's hands
finger ends ingrained with dirt
permanently stained from work
ignoring pain and scorning hurt.

I once saw him walk boldly up to a swan
that had landed in next door's drive and
    wouldn't move.
The police were there because swans are a
    protected species
but didn't do anything, but my dad walked
    up to it,
picked it up and carried it away. No problem.
Those massive wings that can break a man's
    bones
were held tight, tight by my father's hands
and I was proud of him that day, really proud.

Father's hands
tough as leather on old boots
firmly grasping nettle shoots
pulling thistles by their roots.

Father's hands
gripping like an iron vice
never numb in snow and ice
nails and screws are pulled and prised.

He once found a kestrel with a broken wing
and kept it in our garage until it was better.
He'd feed it by hand with scraps of meat or dead
        mice
and you could see where its beak and talons
had taken bits of skin from his finger ends.
It never seemed to hurt him at all, he just smiled
as he let it claw and peck.

Father's hands
lifting bales of hay and straw
calloused, hardened, rough and raw
building, planting, painting . . . more.

Father's hands
hard when tanning my backside
all we needed they supplied
and still my hands will fit inside

Father's hands
large like frying pans
broad as shovel blades
strong as weathered spades.

And still my hands will fit inside
my father's hands.

Paul Cookson

The Way Things Are

No, the candle is not crying, it cannot feel pain.
Even telescopes, like the rest of us, grow bored.
Bubblegum will not make the hair soft and
    shiny.
The duller the imagination, the faster the car,
I am your father and this is the way things are.

When the sky is looking the other way,
do not enter the forest. No, the wind
is not caused by the rushing of clouds.
An excuse is as good a reason as any.
A lighthouse, launched, will not go far,
I am your father and this is the way things are.

No, old people do not walk slowly
because they have plenty of time.
Gardening books when buried will not flower.
Though lightly worn, a crown may leave a scar,
I am your father and this is the way things are.

No, the red woolly hat has not been
put on the railing to keep it warm.
When one glove is missing, both are lost.
Today's craft fair is tomorrow's car boot sale.
The guitarist gently weeps, not the guitar,
I am your father and this is the way things are.

Pebbles work best without batteries.
The deckchair will fail as a unit of currency.
Even though your shadow is shortening
it does not mean you are growing smaller.
Moonbeams sadly, will not survive in a jar,
I am your father and this is the way things are.

For centuries the bullet remained quietly
        confident
that the gun would be invented.
A drowning surrealist will not appreciate
the concrete lifebelt
No guarantee my last goodbye is au revoir,
I am your father and this is the way things are.

Do not become a prison-officer unless you know
what you're letting someone else in for.
The thrill of being a shower curtain will soon
        pall.
No trusting hand awaits the falling star,
I am your father, and I am sorry,
but this is the way things are.

Roger McGough

Let No One Steal Your Dreams

Let no one steal your dreams
Let no one tear apart
The burning of ambition
That fires the drive inside your heart.

Let no one steal your dreams
Let no one tell you that you can't
Let no one hold you back
Let no one tell you that you won't.

Set your sights and keep them fixed
Set your sights on high
Let no one steal your dreams
Your only limit is the sky.

Let no one steal your dreams
Follow your heart
Follow your soul
For only when you follow them
Will you feel truly whole

Set your sights and keep them fixed
Set your sets on high
Let no one steal your dreams
Your only limit is the sky.

Paul Cookson

True Confessions

I've *never* dived for pearls in coral seas,
I've *never* combed gorillas for their fleas,
I've *never* ever surfed on a southerly breeze,
And I've *never* tried to swing on a flying
    trapeze.
But—
I *have* collected honey from a hive of bees,
And I have to admit that I *have* talked to trees,
I have sometimes even succumbed to jealousies,
And I *have* made occasional enemies.

I've *never* found a pirate's treasure chest,
And I've *never* tried to climb Mount Everest,
I've *never* shot an albatross through its breast,
And I've *never*, yet, been under police arrest.
But—
I *have* been under surveillance in Bucharest,
And I *once* robbed a bird of an egg from her
    nest,
I've learnt that things can turn out for the best,
But I've been on several marches to protest.

I've *never* tried to fish in a mackerel sky,
I've *never* sung a frog a lullaby,
I've *never* been to court to testify,
And I've *never* seen the truth with the naked
    eye.
But—
I *have* flapped my arms in the hope I would fly,
And I *have* thoughtlessly made some people cry,
I *have*—sometimes—told a terrible lie,
And I've actually seen somebody close to me
    die.

There are things I'll never do, it's the same
    old song,
There are things I still could, if they're not
    left too long;
There are things I have done which were
    just plain wrong,
And things that happened to me and
    have made me strong.

Sandy Brownjohn

It Ain't What You Do
It's What It Does To You

I have not bummed across America
with only a dollar to spare, one pair
of busted Levi's and a bowie knife.
I have lived with thieves in Manchester.

I have not padded through the Taj Mahal,
barefoot, listening to the space between
each footfall picking up and putting down
its print against the marble floor. But I

skimmed flat stones across Black Moss on a day
so still I could hear each set of ripples
as they crossed. I felt each stone's inertia
spend itself against the water; then sink.

I have not toyed with a parachute chord
while perched on the lip of a light-aircraft;
but I held the wobbly head of a boy
at the day centre, and stroked his fat hands.

And I guess that the tightness in the throat
and the tiny cascading sensation
somewhere inside us are both part of that
sense of something else. That feeling, I mean.

Simon Armitage

Who Knows?

Who knows
How many stars
Are in the roof of the sky?
How many fishes
In the deep seas?
How many people
In the whole wide world?
Who knows
Where, every evening
The sun flees to?
Where the moon lights up?
Where dawn starts,
Where the endless horizon ends,
Who knows? . . . Who knows?

Fatou Ndiaye Sow

Silver Threads

Together we built a palace
mahal
domes and minarets
tiny blue tiles and mirrors.

Wandered
hand in hand
warm feet
on cool floors.

Ran up stairs to call
from towers piercing skies.

Rushed through gardens
pomegranates and white flowers
ruby sweet pungent scent.

Trailed feet in fountained water
and when night fell
argued how many stars
embroidered the sky.

Sari like folds from the heavens
to drape us
liquid blue chiffon
and silver threads

we lay and unthreaded.
How rich we were
silver knots
untied piled high.

It was whilst i was lying thus
stars in my hands

and the heavens
on my lap

that you left.
i searched among the reams
of translucent hope
fearing at first that you had been smothered

or like a baby
choked on a silver thing.

i searched our palace for years
Until
no longer ours
it became mine

all hope lost
single voice ringing
echoes returned
thrown from wall to wall

i gathered our treasure and hid them in my purse

silver bits
spangled love

proof that i had not dreamed alone.

Shamshad Khan

red flowers

red flowers
I saw on a silk tree
in the daytime
turn into my heart's desire
and haunt my mind at night.

Miya Shūji

Bump!

Things that go 'bump' in the night
Should not really give one a fright.
It's the hole in each ear
That lets in the fear,
That, and the absence of light!

Spike Milligan

Face to Face

When I was young what frightened me
Was not the dark,
Was not the shadows on the wall,
Was not the night enclosing all,
Was not the park
Where strangers hid behind each tree.

When I was young what frightened me
Was on the pier—
The Laughing Sailor in his case
With wheezing laugh and sinister face
And sideways leer.
A penny bought this jollity.

Or was my mirror image where
My own eyes
Would stare me back and take control
I seemed to see inside my soul
The hidden lies,
And like a stranger laid them bare.

But now what frightens me the most?
It is the dark,
It is the shadows on the wall,
The night that must enclose us all;
It is the stark
Stranger hidden behind each ghost.

Sandy Brownjohn

Nobody at the Window

School's done.
It's 'See you tomorrow, Goodbye!' to the others,
And then off home
Some of them wait behind to be fetched by their
      mothers,
But mine is at home.
At the end of the long cold street
Grey with the coming of dusk and a splatter of sleet
In a town turning dark at the edges,
There's tea,
And light and the warmth of a fire,
And the family waiting for me
To tell them all that I've done since I went away
(This morning ever so long ago)
– And the dark shut out.

I give a shout,
And run through the slithering wind
And the speckles of sleet –
Past the lamp-post, the door in the wall, the hedge,
And home.

What's happened?
The gate swings wide.
No one at the window to wave –
Is no one inside?
Nobody in the garden,
Nobody at the door –
Don't we even live here any more?
They didn't say they'd be out.
But the front room's as dark as the street,
Uncurtained and cold.

I run up the empty path with a stitch in my side.
Oh there! At the side of the house a streak of gold,
And the back room curtained,
Aglow.
I remember now . . .
They said they'd be there tonight.
What a silly I've been.
Everything's right after all.
Everybody's in.

Margaret Greaves

Objectivity

On a dark night
Only when you turn the light out
in your room
Can you see beyond
the window pane.

Mahood Jamal

Life Doesn't Frighten Me

Shadows on the wall
Noises down the hall
Life doesn't frighten me at all
Bad dogs barking loud
Big ghosts in a cloud
Life doesn't frighten me at all.

Mean old Mother Goose
Lions on the loose
They don't frighten me at all
Dragons breathing flame
On my counterpane
That doesn't frighten me at all.

I go boo
Make them shoo
I make fun
Way them run
I won't cry
So they fly
I just smile
They go wild
Life doesn't frighten me at all.

Tough guys in a fight
All alone at night
Life doesn't frighten me at all.
Panthers in the park
Strangers in the dark
No, they don't frighten me at all.

That new classroom where
Boys all pull my hair
(Kissy little girls
With their hair in curls)
They don't frighten me at all.

Don't show me frogs and snakes
And listen for my screams,
If I'm afraid at all
It's only in my dreams.

I've got a magic charm
That I keep up my sleeve,
I can walk the ocean floor
And never have to breathe.

Life doesn't frighten me at all
Not at all
Not at all
Life doesn't frighten me at all.

Maya Angelou

Yes But Sometimes

Yes. But sometimes I wake in the night,
For a long time, it seems.
And everyone in the house is asleep
And I can't get rid of my dreams.

And the curtains are not quite still,
And lights slide across the ceiling,
And I hear the voice of my own heart.
It's a peculiar feeling.

My thoughts get more and more muddled
And I feel as if I'm falling, falling
Into the dark. And I suppose I sleep;
Because next thing I hear Mum calling.

Gerard Benson

Migraine

Here it comes again: vision bevel-edged
with rainbows, stuff dissolving even as I look
to liquid light, the firm world swimming
just beyond the rim of things.

There's a remedy today: the *migraleve*
they gave me from her medicine cupboard,
I being the daughter who'd inherited this,
and her skin, and the early grey in our hair.

It's the last thing I should be doing,
squinting at a screen at the still centre,
getting the words down before the onset
of vertigo and steel drums.

Then all I'll want is the green curtains drawn
in her room in the afternoon, sun-arrows
    splintering
her dressing table to a clutter of brushes and
    combs,
dusting of powder, its lipsticks and eau de
    cologne.

And her duck-down pillows and old-rose
   eiderdown,
her hand weightless and cool on my brow,
changing the scalding flannel for the cold one.
'A sick headache', they called it, when I was an
   infant.

She taught me to lie so still, the pain wouldn't
   find me.
If I drifted to sleep, she would creep away,
lifting her cool hand
too lightly to wake me.

Gillian Clarke

The Breath of Death
(the cigarette)

This cigarette of which i light
Crisp as death as dark as night
Its tacky smoke will stick to my guts
It makes the food i eat taste like cigarette butts

My breath smells like an ash tray
Cccccan i stop smoking fifteen a day

This cigarette defies my will,
Like my history, to survive

But still
i play with pure death
How long can i sustain life
i died with stale breath

And cancer laughs at my heart
Eats me away till i fall apart
Grabs my fingers and changes the colour
The smell that lingers is death brother

And cancer laughs again you will PAY
Can you stop smoking fifteen a day?

Lemn Sissay

For a Woman with a Fatal Illness

The verdict has been given and you lie quietly
Beyond hope, hate, revenge, even self-pity.

You accept gratefully the gifts—flowers, fruit—
Clumsily offered now that your visitors too

Know you must certainly die in a matter of months,
They are dumb now, reduced only to gestures,

Helpless before your news, perhaps hating
You because you are the cause of their unease.

I, too, watching from my temporary corner,
Feel impotent and wish for something violent—

Whether as sympathy only, I am not sure—
But something at least to break the terrible tension.

Death has no right to come so quietly.

Elizabeth Jennings

Lovebirds

So she moved into hospital the last nine days
to tend him with little strokes and murmurs
as he sank into the sheets. Nurse
set out a low bed for her, night-times, next to his.
He nuzzled up to her as she brushed
away the multiplying cells with a sigh,
was glad as she ignored the many
effluents and the tang of death. The second
last morning of his life he opened
his eyes, saying, 'I can't wake up'
but wouldn't close them for his nap
until he was sure she was there.
Later he moved quietly to deeper sleep
as Professor said he would, still listening
to her twittering on and on until the last.

Jo Shapcott

Come From That Window Child

For Pat Rodney and her children, and the other
thousands in whom Walter Rodney* lives on

Come from that window child
no use looking for daddy tonight
daddy not coming home tonight

Come from that window child
all you'll see is stars burning bright
you won't ever see daddy car light

Come from that window child
in your heart I know you asking why
in my heart too I wish the news was lie

Come from that window child
tonight I feel the darkness bleed
can't tell flower from seed

Come from that window child
to live for truth ain't no easy fight
when some believe power is their right

Come from that window child
a bomb blow up daddy car tonight
but daddy words still burning bright

Come from that window child
tonight you turn a man before your time
tonight you turn a man before your time

John Agard

* Walter Rodney, a Guyanese historian and revolutionary and author of *How Europe Underdeveloped Africa*, was killed on 13 October 1980 in Guyana.

Funeral Blues

Stop all the clocks, cut off the telephone,
Prevent the dog from barking with a juicy bone,
Silence the pianos and with muffled drum
Bring out the coffin, let the mourners come.

Let aeroplanes circle moaning overhead
Scribbling on the sky the message He Is Dead,
Put crêpe bows round the white necks of the
    public doves,
Let the traffic policemen wear black cotton
    gloves.

He was my North, my South, my East and West,
My working week and my Sunday rest,
My noon, my midnight, my talk, my song;
I thought that love would last forever: I was
    wrong.

The stars are not wanted now: put out every one;
Pack up the moon and dismantle the sun;
Pour away the ocean and sweep up the wood;
For nothing now can ever come to any good.

W. H. Auden

The Richest Poor Man
in the Valley

On the outside
he seemed older than he was.
His face was like a weather map
full of bad weather
while inside
his heart was fat with sun.

With his two dogs
he cleared a thin silver path
across the Black Mountain.
And when winter
kicked in
they brought his sheep
down from the top
like sulky clouds.

Harry didn't care for things
that other people prize
like money, houses, bank accounts
and lies.
He was living in a caravan
until the day he died.

But at his funeral
his friends' tears
felt like a thousand
diamonds.

Lindsay MacRae

After the Funeral

The widow stands at the door
and leans her head against the wall.
All is quiet.
The guests are fed
and mostly gone,
and the sea and the town are grey, grey,
with the fishing boats silently putting out.
She hears the talk of the women in the kitchen
and the old men with their drams
discussing a life well lived.
'It's kind of been a happy day,'
she says, looking at her boys,
each with his something
of his father in his face.

Suddenly the sun stabs out bars
of lemon-yellow light
over the fields of glowering corn,
dragons of mist are whisked up
and away across the bay,
and as she turns back to the house
you can still see in her face
the dead man's love for it all.

Meg Bateman

The Old Deaths

In the Twenties, when I was ten or more,
my mother used to tell me about the deaths of
     old people –
perhaps this was to forestall questions like:
'Why don't we go to see Aunt Annie any more?'

She would say, 'You remember old Mrs
     Something?
Well, she's died.' There were never any details –
as now, being grown-up, we might easily say
'It was cancer of the larynx,' or something of the
     something.

I never asked. I wasn't very curious.
Dying, like smoking, was a thing that grown-ups
     did.
Let them get on with it, would be roughly my
     attitude.
I accepted it as part of life; it wasn't odd or
     curious.

Aunt Annie lived close, among Eastern souvenirs –
she had quite a big ivory temple or pagoda,
kept under glass. She was nice, and gave me chocolates.
She was small, like Queen Victoria. Such thoughts are souvenirs,

they are talismans and tokens; not emotional rememberings.
These were the lives I scarcely touched, I brushed against them.
Perhaps I was aware of an atmosphere of kindness –
an old arthritic lady, in a chair, among rememberings.

Gavin Ewart

For Andrew

'Will I die?' you ask. And so I enter on
The dutiful exposition of that which you
Would rather not know, and I rather not tell you.
To soften my 'Yes' I offer compensations –
Age and fulfilment ('it's so far away;
You will have children and grandchildren by then')
And indifference ('By then you will not care').
No need: you cannot believe me, convinced
That if you always eat plenty of vegetables
And are careful crossing the street you will live
        for ever.
And so we close the subject, with much unsaid –
This, for instance: Though you and I may die
Tomorrow or next year, and nothing remain
Of our stock, of the unique, preciously-hoarded
Inimitable genes we carry in us,
It is possible that for many generations

There will exist, sprung from whatever seeds,
Children straight-limbed, with clear enquiring voices,
Bright-eyed as you. Or so I like to think:
Sharing in this your childish optimism.

Fleur Adcock

Do not write poems about your father's death

the well-known poet said,
and especially not also several other kinds of poem
of the sort I try to write.

And as I took the bus home
—wondering was the driver's dad dead—
I thought what is it all about,
this influential advice dripping on my page,
this top-writer talk tippexing out
things I've thought?

Well what it is, I decided
is groan-up literary readers
who've been to the university
a lot not to mention poetry readings
deciding we ought to write about
capital I Important Things—Wars, Plagues,
Famines, the Environment, the Millennium

etc not just frogs and tadpoles,
ailing hamsters, bawling babies,
football, old buses, bats, birds
Tom and Jerry cartoons, cornflakes,
bad refs, sudden deaths, and all
the other un-

Important things I'll go on writing about
including bus-drivers whose dads
might be alive

and snotty poets.

Robert Hull

Remember

Remember me when I am gone away,
    Gone far away into the silent land;
    When you can no more hold me by the hand,
Nor I half turn to go yet turning stay.
Remember me when no more day by day
    You tell me of our future that you planned:
    Only remember me; you understand
It will be late to counsel then or pray.
Yet if you should forget me for a while
    And afterwards remember, do not grieve:
    For if the darkness and corruption leave
A vestige of the thoughts that once I had,
Better by far you should forget and smile
    Than that you should remember and be sad.

Christina Rossetti

Postscript for Gweno

If I should go away,
Beloved, do not say
'He has forgotten me.'
For you abide,
A singing rib within my dreaming side;
You always stay.

And in the mad tormented valley
Where blood and hunger rally
And Death the wild beast is uncaught, untamed,
Our soul withstands the terror
And has its quiet honour
Among the glittering stars your voices named.

Alun Lewis

After You'd Gone

No one
like you.
That then
the pleasure.
That now
the pain.

Steve Turner

Dunblane
13 March 1996

Dear Lord, help me.
The Minister says that I shall
Hear my friends' voices in the wind of morning.
That their small hands will touch my own with
the evening breeze.
He says that their tears shall fall as gentle rain
on my face,
and their gift of laughter warm me with the sun.
The Minister says that my friends
will walk with me in the wakeful light of dawn,
and that the sound of the names will be a song forever
for sparrows in the playground,
(whatever *that* means).
But Lord,
why can't they play hopscotch with me
on Thursdays?

Lucy Coats

The Crying Game

Crying at airports when loved ones come home
Tears of relief that you're not left alone
Watching a soap, letting out a loud bawl
When the star in a coma doesn't die after all

Sniffling at weddings as love walks the aisle
And joy like confetti covers all in a smile
Christmas morn blubbing when you're given a pet
Sobbing at Wembley when your team finds the net

Weeping with laughter at a video clip
When a showing-off father loses his grip
Makes a bum-first-splash-landing, one of life's sports
A tarzan, whose rope broke, in pot-bellied shorts

Where do tears come from, some underskin vault?
These flash floods of feelings we can't seem to halt
These wordless expressions that leak down our
        cheek
Perhaps it's the heart longing to speak.

Stewart Henderson

Goodbye

He said
goodbye.
I shuffled
my feet
and kept a close
watch on my
shoes.
He was talking
I was listening
but he probably
thought I was
not
because I never
even lifted my
head.
I didn't want him
to see
the mess mascara
makes when it
runs.

Carole-Ann Marsh

Love Note

when I know you're going away
I miss you before you've even gone

Adrian Mitchell

Weeping World

There is a time of weeping and there is a time of laughing. But as you see, he setteth the weeping time before, for that is the time of this wretched world and the laughing time shall come after in heaven. There is also a time of sowing, and a time of reaping too. Now must we in this world sow, that we may in the other world reap: and in this short sowing time of this weeping world, must we water our seed with the showers of our tears, and then shall we have in heaven a merry laughing harvest for ever.

Sir Thomas More

Index of first lines

Don't Panic! 163

Don't Panic! 165

List of poets

Don't Panic! 169

Acknowledgements

The compiler and publishers wish to thank the following for permission to use copyright material:

Fleur Adcock, 'For Andrew' from *Poems 1960-2000* by Fleur Adcock (2000), by permission of Bloodaxe Books; **John Agard**, 'Come From That Window Child' from *Mangoes and Bullets* by John Agard, Serpent's Tail (1990); and 'Spell to Banish a Pimple' from *Get Back Pimple* by John Agard, Puffin (1997), by permission of Caroline Sheldon Literary Agency on behalf of the author; **Maya Angelou**, 'Life Doesn't Frighten Me' from *And Still I Rise* by Maya Angelou, Virago (1978). Copyright © 1978 by Maya Angelou by permission of Time Warner Books UK and Random House, Inc; **Simon Armitage**, 'It Ain't What You Do' from *Zoom* by Simon Armitage (1989), by permission of Bloodaxe Books; **W. H. Auden**, 'Funeral Blues' from *Collected Poems*, by permission of Faber and Faber Ltd; **Meg Bateman**, 'After the Funeral' from *Lightness and Other Poems*, Polygon, by permission of Birlinn Ltd; **Gerard Benson**, 'Yes But Sometimes' by permission of The Poetry Business; **Valerie Bloom**, 'I Hope Tomorrow Never Comes' from *The World is Sweet*, Bloomsbury (2000), by permission of the author; **Sandy Brownjohn**, 'True Confessions' and 'Face to Face' from *In*

renewed 1964 by Carl Sandburg, by permission of Harcourt, Inc; **Carole Satyamurti**, 'Broken Moon' from *Selected Poems* by Carole Satyamurti (2000), by permission of Bloodaxe Books; **Jo Shapcott**, 'Lovebirds' from *Her Book* by Jo Shapcott, by permission of Faber and Faber; **Miya Shūji**, 'red flowers' from *Gunkei* (1946) included in *Modern Japanese Tanka*, ed. Makoto Ueda (1996), by permission of Columbia University Press; **Matthew Sweeney**, 'Smile' from *Fatso in the Red Suit* by Matthew Sweeney (1995), by permission of Faber and Faber; **Veronique Tadjo**, 'Friendship' from *Talking Drums*, ed. Veronique Tadjo, by permission of A & C Black Publishers Ltd; **Steve Turner**, 'After You'd Gone', 'Depression' and 'The Mirror' from *Poems* by Steve Turner (2002); and 'My Room' from *The Moon Has Got Its Pants On* by Steve Turner (2001), by permission of Lion Publishing; **Jim Wong-Chu**, 'Equal Opportunity' from *Chinatown Ghosts* (1986), by permission of Arsenal Pulp Press.

Every effort has been made to trace the copyright holders but if any have been inadvertently overlooked the publishers will be pleased to make the necessary arrangement at the first opportunity.

L^oVe

Poems chosen by FIONA WATERS

Wishing for it, waiting for it, being in it,
falling out of it, finding it, losing it,
longing for it, grieving for it . . .
From silent admiration to great dramatic
Passion, every aspect of love can be found
within the pages of this little book.

Included are poems by Carol Ann Duffy, Wendy Cope,
C. Day Lewis, Adrian Henri, Roger McGough, Dorothy
Parker, Spike Milligan, John Betjeman, W. H. Auden
and Noel Coward, to name but a few.

Golden Apples

Poems for Children chosen by FIONA WATERS

In this treasure chest of verse, there are poems old and new.
Poems from W. B. Yeats, John Betjeman, Robert Louis
Stevenson, Roger McGough, Charles Causley and Walter de
la Mare to name but a few. There is humour, mystery, joy
and sadness in this small world of poetry which introduces
the pleasure of poetry of all kinds.

The Fox on the Roundabout

Poems by GARETH OWEN

A new edition of Gareth Owen's classic collection, *The Fox on the Roundabout*, which features some of his wittiest, funniest and most poignant poetry, including six fantastic brand-new poems. Gareth Owen's bitter-sweet observations on life and the world will strike a chord with readers everywhere.